THE GALAPAGOS ISLANDS

CHARLES DARWIN

THE GALAPAGOS ISLANDS

PENGUIN BOOKS

PENGUIN BOOKS
Published by the Penguin Group
Penguin Books USA Inc., 375 Hudson Street,
New York, New York 10014, U.S.A.
Penguin Books Ltd, 27 Wrights Lane,
London W8 5TZ, England
Penguin Books Australia Ltd, Ringwood,
Victoria, Australia
Penguin Books Canada Ltd, 10 Alcorn Avenue,
Toronto, Ontario, Canada M4V 3B2
Penguin Books (N.Z.) Ltd, 182–190 Wairau Road,
Auckland 10, New Zealand

Penguin Books Ltd, Registered Offices:
Harmondsworth, Middlesex, England

Published in Penguin Books 1995

This extract is from *Voyage of the Beagle,* edited and introduced
by Janet Browne and Michael Neue, published by Penguin Books.

ISBN 0 14 60.0144 3

Printed in the United States of America

CONTENTS

Galapagos Archipelago

Islands volcanic – Number of craters – Leafless
bushes – Colony at Charles Island – James Island – Salt-lake in
crater – Character of vegetation – Ornithology, curious finches –
Great tortoises, habits of, paths to the wells – Marine lizard feeds
on sea-weed – Terrestrial species, burrowing habits, herbivorous –
Importance of reptiles in the archipelago – Few and minute
insects – American type of organization – Species confined
to certain islands – Tameness of birds – Falkland Islands –
Fear of man an acquired instinct

SEPTEMBER 15TH – The *Beagle* arrived at the southern-most of the Galapagos Islands. This archipelago consists of ten principal islands, of which five much exceed the others in size. They are situated under the equatorial line, and between 500 and 600 miles to the westward of the coast of America. The constitution of the whole is volcanic. With the exception of some ejected fragments of granite, which have been most curiously glazed and altered by the heat, every part consists of lava, or of sandstone resulting from the attrition of such materials. The higher islands (which attain an elevation of 3,000, and even 4,000 feet) generally have one or more principal craters towards their centre, and on their flanks smaller orifices. I have no exact data from which to calculate, but I do not hesitate to affirm, that there must be, in all the islands of the archipelago, at least 2,000 craters. These are of two kinds; one, as in ordinary cases, consisting of scoriæ and lava, the other of finely stratified volcanic sandstone. The latter in most instances have a form beautifully symmetrical: their origin is due to the ejection of mud – that is, fine volcanic ashes and water – without any lava.

Considering that these islands are placed directly under the equator, the climate is far from being excessively hot; a circumstance which, perhaps, is chiefly owing to the singularly low temperature of the surrounding sea. Excepting during one short season, very little rain falls, and even then it is not regular: but the clouds generally hang low. From these circumstances the lower parts of the islands are extremely arid, whilst the summits, at an elevation of 1,000 feet or more, possess a tolerably luxuriant vegetation. This is especially the case on the windward side, which first receives and condenses the moisture from the atmosphere.

In the morning (17th) we landed on Chatham Island, which, like the others, rises with a tame and rounded outline, interrupted only here and there by scattered hillocks – the remains of former craters. Nothing could be less inviting than the first appearance. A broken field of black basaltic lava is every where covered by a stunted brushwood, which shows little signs of life. The dry and parched surface, having been heated by the noonday sun, gave the air a close and sultry feeling, like that from a stove: we fancied even the bushes smelt unpleasantly. Although I diligently tried to collect as many plants as possible, I succeeded in getting only ten kinds; and such wretched-looking little weeds would have better become an arctic, than an equatorial Flora.

The thin woods, which cover the lower parts of all the islands, excepting where the lava has recently flowed, appear from a short distance quite leafless, like the deciduous trees of the northern hemisphere in winter. It was some time before I discovered, that not only almost every plant was in full leaf, but that the greater number were now in flower. After the period of heavy rains, the islands are said to appear for a short time partially green. The only other country, in which I have seen a vegetation with a character at all approaching to this, is at the volcanic island of Fernando Noronha, placed in many respects under similar conditions.

The natural history of this archipelago is very remarkable: it seems to be a little world within itself, the greater number of its inhabitants, both vegetable and animal, being found nowhere else. As I shall refer to this subject again, I will only here remark, as forming a striking character on first landing, that the birds are strangers to man. So tame and unsuspecting were they, that they did not even understand what was meant by stones being thrown at them; and quite regardless of us, they approached so close that any number might have been killed with a stick.

The *Beagle* sailed round Chatham Island, and anchored in several bays. One night I slept on shore, on a part of the

3

island where some black cones – the former chimneys of the subterranean heated fluids – were extraordinarily numerous. From one small eminence, I counted sixty of these truncated hillocks, which were all surmounted by a more or less perfect crater. The greater number consisted merely of a ring of red scoriæ, or slags, cemented together: and their height above the plain of lava, was not more than from 50 to 100 feet. From their regular form, they gave the country a *workshop* appearance, which strongly reminded me of those parts of Staffordshire where the great iron-foundries are most numerous.

The age of the various beds of lava was distinctly marked by the comparative growth, or entire absence, of vegetation. Nothing can be imagined more rough and horrid than the surface of the more modern streams. These have been aptly compared to the sea petrified in its most boisterous moments: no sea, however, would present such irregular undulations, or would be traversed by such deep chasms. All the craters are in an extinct condition; and although the age of the different streams of lava could be so clearly distinguished, it is probable they have remained so for many centuries. There is no account in any of the old voyagers of any volcano on this island having been seen in activity; yet since the time of Dampier (1684), there must have been some increase in the quantity of vegetation, otherwise so accurate a person would not have expressed himself thus: 'Four or five of the easternmost islands are rocky, barren, and hilly, producing neither tree, herb, nor grass, but a few dildoe (cactus) trees, except by the seaside.' This description is at present applicable only to the western islands, where the volcanic forces are in frequent activity.

The day, on which I visited the little craters, was glowing hot, and the scrambling over the rough surface, and through the intricate thickets, was very fatiguing; but I was well repaid by the Cyclopian scene. In my walk I met two large tortoises, each of which must have weighed at least 200 pounds. One was eating a piece of cactus, and when I approached, it looked at me, and then quietly walked away: the other gave a deep hiss and drew in its head. These huge reptiles, surrounded by the black lava, the leafless shrubs, and large cacti, appeared to my fancy like some antediluvian animals.

SEPTEMBER 23RD – The *Beagle* proceeded to Charles Island. This archipelago has long been frequented, first by the bucaniers, and latterly by whalers, but it is only within the last six years, that a small colony has been established on it. The inhabitants are between 200 and 300 in number: they nearly all consist of people of colour, who have been banished for political crimes from the Republic of the Equator (Quito is the capital of this state) to which these islands belong. The settlement is placed about four and a half miles inland, and at an elevation probably of 1,000 feet. In the first part of the road we passed through leafless thickets, as in Chatham Island. Higher up, the wood gradually became greener; and immediately we had crossed the ridge of the island, our bodies were cooled by the fine southerly trade wind, and our senses refreshed by the sight of a green and thriving vegetation. The houses are irregularly scattered over a flat space of ground, which is cultivated with sweet potatoes and bananas. It will not easily be imagined how pleasant the sight of black mud was to us, after having been so long accustomed to the parched soil of Peru and Chile.

The inhabitants, although complaining of poverty, gain, without much trouble, the means of subsistence from the fertile soil. In the woods there are many wild pigs and goats, but the main article of animal food is derived from the tortoise. Their numbers in this island have of course been greatly reduced, but the people yet reckon on two days' hunting supplying food for the rest of the week. It is said that formerly single vessels have taken away as many as 700 of these animals, and that the ship's company of a frigate some years since brought down 200 to the beach in one day.

We stayed at this island four days, during which time I collected many plants and birds. One morning I ascended the highest hill, which has an altitude of nearly 1,800 feet. The summit consists of a broken-down crater, thickly clothed with coarse grass and brushwood. Even in this one island, I counted thirty-nine hills, each of which was terminated by a more or less perfect circular depression.

SEPTEMBER 29TH – We doubled the south-west extremity

of Albemarle Island and the next day were nearly becalmed between it and Narborough Island. Both are covered with immense streams of black naked lava; which, having either flowed over the rims of the great caldrons, or having burst forth from the smaller orifices on the flanks, have in their descent spread over miles of the sea-coast. On both of these islands eruptions are known occasionally to take place; and in Albemarle we saw a small jet of smoke curling from the summit of one of the more lofty craters. In the evening we anchored in Bank's Cove, in Albemarle Island.

When morning came, we found that the harbour in which we were at anchor was formed by a broken-down crater, composed of volcanic sandstone. After breakfast I went out walking. To the southward of this first crater, there was another of similar composition, and beautifully symmetrical. It was elliptic in form; the longer axis being less than a mile, and its depth about 500 feet. The bottom was occupied by a shallow lake, and in its centre a tiny crater formed an islet. The day was overpoweringly hot, and the lake looked clear and blue. I hurried down the cindery slope, and choked with dust eagerly tasted the water – but to my sorrow I found it salt as brine.

The rocks on the coast abounded with great black lizards, between 3 and 4 feet long; and on the hills, another species was equally common. We saw several of the latter, some clumsily running out of our way, and others shuffling into their burrows. I shall presently describe in more detail the habits of both these reptiles.

OCTOBER 3RD – We sailed round the northern end of Albemarle Island. Nearly the whole of this side is covered with recent streams of dark-coloured lavas, and is studded with craters. I should think it would be difficult to find in any other part of the world, an island situated within the tropics, and of such considerable size (namely 75 miles long), so sterile and incapable of supporting life.

On the 8th we reached James Island. Captain FitzRoy put Mr Bynoe, myself, and three others on shore, leaving with us a tent and provisions, to wait there till the vessel returned from watering. This was an admirable plan for the collections, as we had an entire week of hard work. We found here a party of Spaniards, who had been sent from Charles Island to dry fish, and to salt tortoise-meat.

At the distance of about 6 miles, and at the height of nearly 2,000 feet, the Spaniards had erected a hovel in which two men lived, who were employed in catching tortoises, whilst the others were fishing on the coast. I paid this party two visits, and slept there one night. In the same manner as in the other islands, the lower region is covered by nearly leafless bushes: but here many of them grow to the size of trees. I measured several which were 2 feet in diameter, and some even 2 feet 9 inches. The upper region being kept damp, from the moisture of the condensed clouds, supports a green and flourishing vegetation. So damp was the ground, that there were large beds of a

8

coarse carex, in which great numbers of a very small water-rail lived and bred. While staying in this upper region, we lived entirely upon tortoise-meat. The breast-plate roasted (as the Gauchos do *carne con cuero*), with the flesh attached to it, is very good; and the young tortoises make excellent soup; but otherwise the meat to my taste is very indifferent.

During another day we accompanied a party of the Spaniards in their whale-boat to a salina, or lake from which salt is procured. After landing, we had a very rough walk over a rugged field of recent lava, which has almost surrounded a sandstone crater, at the bottom of which the salt-lake is situated. The water was only 3 or 4 inches deep, and rested on a layer of beautifully crystallized white salt. The lake was quite circular, and fringed with a border of brightly green succulent plants: the precipitous walls of the crater were also clothed with wood, so that the scene was both picturesque and curious. A few years since, the sailors belonging to a sealing-vessel murdered their captain in this quiet spot; and we saw his skull lying among the bushes.

During the greater part of our week on shore, the sky was cloudless, and if the trade wind failed for an hour, the heat became very oppressive. On two days, the thermo-meter within the tent stood for some hours at 93°; but in the open air, in the wind and sun, at only 85°. The sand was extremely hot; the thermometer placed in some of a brown colour immediately rose to 137°, and how much higher it would have risen, I do not know, for it was not graduated above that number. The *black* sand felt much hotter, so that even in thick boots it was disagreeable, on this account, to walk over it.

I will now offer a few general observations on the natural history of these islands. I endeavoured to make as nearly a perfect collection in every branch as time permitted. The plants have not yet been examined, but Professor Henslow, who has kindly undertaken the description of them, informs me that there are probably many new species, and perhaps even some new genera. They all have an extremely weedy character, and it would scarcely have been supposed, that they had grown at an inconsiderable elevation directly under the equator. In the lower and sterile parts, the bush, which from its minute brown leaves chiefly gives the leafless appearance to the brushwood, is one of the Euphorbiaceæ. In the same region an acacia and a cactus (*Opuntia Galapageia*), with large oval compressed articulations, springing from a cylindrical stem, are in some parts common. These are the only trees which in that part afford any shade. Near the summits of the different islands, the vegetation has a very different character; ferns and coarse grasses are abundant; and the commonest tree is one of the Compositæ. Tree-ferns are not present. One of the most singular characters of the Flora, considering the position of this archipelago, is the absence of every member of the palm family. Cocos Island, on the other hand, which is the nearest point of land, takes its name from the great number of cocoa-nut trees on it. From the presence of the Opuntias and some other plants, the vegetation partakes more of the character of that of America than of any other country.

Of mammalia a large kind of mouse forms a well-marked species. From its large thin ears, and other characters, it approaches in form a section of the genus, which is confined to the sterile regions of South America. There is also a rat which Mr Waterhouse believes is probably distinct from the English kind; but I cannot help suspecting that it is only the same altered by the peculiar conditions of its new country.

In my collections from these islands, Mr Gould considers that there are twenty-six different species of land birds. With the exception of one, all probably are undescribed kinds, which inhabit this archipelago, and no other part of the world. Among the waders and waterfowl it is more difficult, without detailed comparison, to say what are new. But a water-rail which lives near the summits of the mountains, is undescribed, as perhaps is a Totanus and a heron. The only kind of gull which is found among these islands, is also new; when the wandering habits of this genus are considered, this is a very remarkable circumstance. The species most closely allied to it, comes from the Strait of Magellan. Of the other aquatic birds, the species appear the same with well-known American birds.

The general character of the plumage of these birds is extremely plain, and like the Flora possesses little beauty.

Although the species are thus peculiar to the archipelago, yet nearly all in their general structure, habits, colour of feathers, and even tone of voice, are strictly American. The following brief list will give an idea of their kinds. First: A buzzard, having many of the characters of Polyborus or Caracara; and in its habits not to be distinguished from that peculiar South American genus; second: Two owls; third: Three species of tyrant-flycatchers — a form strictly American. One of these appears identical with a common kind (*Muscicapa coronata*? Lath.), which has a very wide range, from La Plata throughout Brazil to Mexico; fourth: A sylvicola, an American form, and especially common in the northern division of the continent; fifth: Three species of mocking-birds, a genus common to both Americas; sixth: A finch, with a stiff tail and a long claw to its hinder toe, closely allied to a North American genus; seventh: A swallow belonging to the American division of that genus; eighth: A dove, like, but distinct from, the Chilean species; ninth: A group of finches, of which Mr Gould considers there are thirteen species; and these he has distributed into four new sub-genera. These birds are the most singular of any in the archipelago. They all agree in many points; namely, in a peculiar structure of their bill, short tails, general form, and in their plumage. The females are grey or brown, but the old cocks jet-black. All the species, excepting two, feed in flocks on the ground, and have very similar habits. It is very remarkable that a nearly perfect gradation of structure in this one group can be traced in the form of the beak, from one exceeding in dimensions that of the largest gros-beak, to another differing but little from that of a warbler. Of the aquatic birds I have already remarked that some are peculiar to these islands, and some common to North and South America.

We will now turn to the order of reptiles, which forms, perhaps, the most striking feature in the zoology of these islands. The species are not numerous, but the number of individuals of each kind, is extraordinarily great. There is one kind both of the turtle and tortoise; of lizards four; and of snakes about the same number.

I will first describe the habits of the tortoise (*Testudo Indicus*) which has been so frequently alluded to. These animals are found, I believe, in all the islands of the archipelago; certainly in the greater number. They frequent in preference the high damp parts, but likewise inhabit the lower and arid districts. I have already mentioned proofs, from the numbers which have been taken in a single day, how very numerous they must be. Some individuals grow to an immense size: Mr Lawson, an Englishman, who had at the time of our visit charge of the colony, told us that he had seen several so large, that it required six or eight men to lift them from the ground; and that some had afforded as much as 200 pounds of meat. The old males are the largest, the females rarely growing to so great a size. The male can readily be distinguished from the female by the greater length of its tail. The tortoises which live on those islands where there is no water, or in the lower and arid parts of the others, chiefly feed on the succulent cactus. Those which frequent the higher and damp regions, eat the leaves of various trees, a kind of berry (called guayavita) which is acid and austere, and likewise a pale green filamentous lichen, that hangs in tresses from the boughs of the trees.

The tortoise is very fond of water, drinking large quantities, and wallowing in the mud. The larger islands alone possess springs, and these are always situated towards the central parts, and at a considerable elevation. The tortoises, therefore, which frequent the lower districts, when thirsty, are obliged to travel from a long distance. Hence broad and well-beaten paths radiate off in every direction from the wells even down to the sea-coast; and the Spaniards, by following them up, first discovered the watering-places. When I landed at Chatham Island, I could not imagine what animal travelled so methodically along the well-chosen tracks. Near the springs it was a curious spectacle to behold many of these great monsters; one set eagerly travelling onwards with outstretched necks, and another set returning, after having drunk their fill. When the tortoise arrives at the spring, quite regardless of any spectator, it buries its head in the water above its eyes, and greedily swallows great mouthfuls, at the rate of about ten in a minute. The inhabitants say each animal stays three or four days in the neighbourhood of the water, and then returns to the lower country; but they differed in their accounts respecting the frequency of these visits. The animal probably regulates them according to the nature of the food which it has consumed. It is, however, certain, that tortoises can subsist even on those islands where there is no other water, than what falls during a few rainy days in the year.

I believe it is well ascertained, that the bladder of the frog acts as a reservoir for the moisture necessary to its existence: such seems to be the case with the tortoise. For some time after a visit to the springs, the urinary bladder of these animals is distended with fluid, which is said gradually to decrease in volume, and to become less pure. The inhabitants, when walking in the lower district, and overcome with thirst, often take advantage of this circumstance, by killing a tortoise, and if the bladder is full, drinking its contents. In one I saw killed, the fluid was quite limpid, and had only a *very slightly* bitter taste. The inhabitants, however, always drink first the water in the pericardium, which is described as being best.

The tortoises, when moving towards any definite point, travel by night and day, and arrive at their journey's end much sooner than would be expected. The inhabitants, from observations on marked individuals, consider that they can move a distance of about 8 miles in two or three days. One large tortoise, which I watched, I found walked at the rate of 60 yards in ten minutes, that is 360 in the hour, or 4 miles a day, allowing also a little time for it to eat on the road.

During the breeding season, when the male and female

are together, the male utters a hoarse roar or bellowing, which, it is said, can be heard at the distance of more than 100 yards. The female never uses her voice, and the male only at such times; so that when the people hear this noise, they know the two are together. They were at this time (October) laying their eggs. The female, where the soil is sandy, deposits them together, and covers them up with sand; but where the ground is rocky she drops them indiscriminately in any hollow. Mr Bynoe found seven placed in a line in a fissure. The egg is white and spherical; one which I measured was seven inches and three-eighths in circumference. The young animals, as soon as they are hatched, fall a prey in great numbers to the buzzard, with the habits of the Caracara. The old ones seem generally to die from accidents, as from falling down precipices. At least several of the inhabitants told me, they had never found one dead without some such apparent cause.

The inhabitants believe that these animals are absolutely deaf; certainly they do not overhear a person walking close behind them. I was always amused, when overtaking one of these great monsters as it was quietly pacing along, to see how suddenly, the instant I passed, it would draw in its head and legs, and uttering a deep hiss fall to the ground with a heavy sound, as if struck dead. I frequently got on their backs, and then, upon giving a few raps on the hinder part of the shell, they would rise up and walk away; but I found it very difficult to keep my balance.

The flesh of this animal is largely employed, both fresh

and salted; and a beautifully clear oil is prepared from the fat. When a tortoise is caught, the man makes a slit in the skin near its tail, so as to see inside its body, whether the fat under the dorsal plate is thick. If it is not, the animal is liberated; and it is said to recover soon from this strange operation. In order to secure the tortoises, it is not sufficient to turn them like turtle, for they are often able to regain their upright position.

It was confidently asserted, that the tortoises coming from different islands in the archipelago were slightly different in form; and that in certain islands they attained a larger average size than in others. Mr Lawson maintained that he could at once tell from which island any one was brought. Unfortunately, the specimens which came home in the *Beagle* were too small to institute any certain comparison. This tortoise, which goes by the name of *Testudo Indicus*, is at present found in many parts of the world. It is the opinion of Mr Bell, and some others who have studied reptiles, that it is not improbable that they all originally came from this archipelago. When it is known how long these islands have been frequented by the bucaniers, and that they constantly took away numbers of these animals alive, it seems very probable that they should have distributed them in different parts of the world. If this tortoise does not originally come from these islands, it is a remarkable anomaly; in as much as nearly all the other land inhabitants seem to have had their birthplace here.

Of lizards there are four or five species; two probably

belong to the South American genus Leiocephalus, and two to Amblyrhyncus. This remarkable genus was characterized by Mr Bell, from a stuffed specimen sent from Mexico, but which I conceive there can be little doubt originally came through some whaling ship from these islands. The two species agree pretty closely in general appearance; but one is aquatic and the other terrestrial in its habits. Mr Bell thus concludes his description of *Amb. cristatus*: 'On a comparison of this animal with the true Iguanas, the most striking and important discrepancy is in the form of the head. Instead of the long, pointed, narrow muzzle of those species, we have here a short, obtusely truncated head, not so long as it is broad, the mouth consequently only capable of being opened to a very short space. These circumstances, with the shortness and equality of the toes, and the strength and curvature of the claws, evidently indicate some striking peculiarity in its food and general habits, on which, however, in the absence of all certain information, I shall abstain from offering any conjecture.' The following account of these two lizards, will, I think, show with what judgment Mr Bell foresaw a variation in habit, accompanying change in structure.

First for the aquatic kind (*Amb. cristatus*). This lizard is extremely common on all the islands throughout the archipelago. It lives exclusively on the rocky sea-beaches, and is never found, at least I never saw one, even 10 yards inshore. It is a hideous-looking creature, of a dirty black colour, stupid and sluggish in its movements. The usual length of a full-grown one is about a yard, but there are some even 4 feet long: I have seen a large one which weighed 20 pounds. On the island of Albemarle they seem to grow to a greater size than on any other. These lizards were occasionally seen some 100 yards from the shore swimming about; and Captain Collnett, in his *Voyage* says, 'they go out to sea in shoals to fish'. With respect to the object, I believe he is mistaken; but the fact stated on such good authority cannot be doubted. When in the water the animal swims with perfect ease and quickness, by a serpentine movement of its body and flattened tail – the legs, during this time, being motionless and closely collapsed on its sides. A seaman on board sank one, with a heavy weight attached to it, thinking thus to kill it directly; but when an hour afterwards he drew up the line, the lizard was quite active. Their limbs and strong claws are admirably adapted for crawling over the rugged and fissured masses of lava, which every where form the coast. In such situations, a group of six or seven of these hideous reptiles may oftentimes be seen on the black rocks, a few feet above the surf, basking in the sun with outstretched legs.

I opened the stomach of several, and in each case found it largely distended with minced sea-weed, of that kind which grows in thin foliaceous expansions of a bright green or dull red colour. I do not recollect having observed this sea-weed in any quantity on the tidal rocks; and I have reason to believe it grows at the bottom of the sea, at some little distance from the coast. If such is the case, the object of these animals occasionally going out to sea is explained. The stomach contained nothing but the sea-weed. Mr Bynoe, however, found a piece of a crab in one; but this might have got in accidentally, in the same manner as I have seen a caterpillar, in the midst of some lichen, in the paunch of a tortoise. The intestines were large, as in other herbivorous animals.

The nature of this lizard's food, as well as the structure of its tail, and the certain fact of its having been seen voluntarily swimming out at sea, absolutely prove its aquatic habits; yet there is in this respect one strange anomaly; namely, that when frightened it will not enter the water. From this cause, it is easy to drive these lizards down to any little point overhanging the sea, where they will sooner allow a person to catch hold of their tail than jump into the water. They do not seem to have any notion of biting; but when much frightened they squirt a drop of fluid from each nostril. One day I carried one to a deep pool left by the retiring tide, and threw it in several times as far as I was able. It invariably returned in a direct line to the spot where I stood. It swam near the bottom, with a very graceful and rapid movement, and occasionally aided itself over the uneven ground with its feet. As soon as it arrived near the margin, but still being under water, it either tried to conceal itself in the tufts of sea-weed, or it entered some crevice. As soon as it thought the danger was past, it crawled out on the dry rocks, and shuffled away as quickly as it could. I several times caught this same lizard, by driving it down to a point, and though possessed of such perfect powers of diving and swimming, nothing would induce it to enter the water; and so often as I threw it in, it returned in the manner above described. Perhaps this singular piece of apparent stupidity may be accounted for by the circumstance, that this reptile has no enemy whatever on shore, whereas at sea it must often fall a prey to the numerous sharks. Hence, probably urged by a fixed and hereditary instinct that the shore is its place of safety, whatever the emergency may be, it there takes refuge.

During our visit (in October) I saw extremely few small individuals of this species, and none I should think under a year old. From this circumstance it seems probable that the breeding season had not commenced. I asked several of the inhabitants if they knew where it laid its eggs: they said, that although well acquainted with the eggs of the other kind, they had not the least knowledge of the manner in which this species is propagated; a fact, considering how common an animal this lizard is, not a little extraordinary.

We will now turn to the terrestrial species (*Amb. sub-cristatus* of Gray). This species, differently from the last, is confined to the central islands of the archipelago, namely to Albemarle, James, Barrington, and Indefatigable. To the southward, in Charles, Hood, and Chatham islands, and to the northward, in Towers, Bindloes, and Abington, I neither saw nor heard of any. It would appear as if this species had been created in the centre of the archipelago, and thence had been dispersed only to a certain distance.

In the central islands they inhabit both the higher and damp, as well as the lower and sterile parts; but in the latter they are much the most numerous. I cannot give a more forcible proof of their numbers, than by stating, that when we were left at James Island, we could not for some time find a spot free from their burrows, on which to pitch our tent. These lizards, like their brothers the sea-kind, are ugly animals; and from their low facial angle have a singularly stupid appearance. In size perhaps they are a little inferior to the latter, but several of them weighed between 10 and 15 pounds each. The colour of their belly, front legs, and head (excepting the crown which is nearly white), is a dirty yellowish-orange: the back is a brownish-red, which in the younger specimens is darker. In their movements they are lazy and half torpid. When not frightened, they slowly crawl along with their tails and bellies dragging on the ground. They often stop, and doze for a minute with closed eyes, and hind legs spread out on the parched soil.

They inhabit burrows; which they sometimes excavate between fragments of lava, but more generally on level patches of the soft volcanic sandstone. The holes do not appear to be very deep, and they enter the ground at a small angle; so that when walking over these lizard *warrens*, the soil is constantly giving way, much to the annoyance of the tired walker. This animal when excavating its burrow, alternately works the opposite sides of its body. One front leg for a short time scratches up the soil, and throws it towards the hind foot, which is well placed so as to heave it beyond the mouth of the hole. This side of the body being tired, the other takes up the task, and so on alternately. I watched one for a long time, till half its body was buried; I then walked up and pulled it by the tail; at this it was greatly astonished, and soon shuffled up to see what was the matter; and then stared me in the face, as much as to say, 'What made you pull my tail?'

They feed by day, and do not wander far from their burrows; and if frightened they rush to them with a most awkward gait. Except when running down hill, they cannot move very fast; which appears chiefly owing to the lateral position of their legs.

They are not at all timorous: when attentively watching any one, they curl their tails, and raising themselves on their front legs, nod their heads vertically, with a quick movement, and try to look very fierce: but in reality they are not at all so; if one just stamps the ground, down go their tails, and off they shuffle as quickly as they can. I have frequently observed small muscivorous lizards, when watching any thing, nod their heads in precisely the same manner; but I do not at all know for what purpose. If this Amblyrhyncus is held, and plagued with a stick, it will bite it very severely; but I caught many by the tail, and they never tried to bite me. If two are placed on the ground and

23

held together, they will fight and bite each other till blood is drawn.

The individuals (and they are the greater number) which inhabit the lower country, can scarcely taste a drop of water throughout the year; but they consume much of the succulent cactus, the branches of which are occasionally broken off by the wind. I have sometimes thrown a piece to two or three when together; and it was amusing enough to see each trying to seize and carry it away in its mouth, like so many hungry dogs with a bone. They eat very deliberately, but do not chew their food. The little birds are aware how harmless these creatures are: I have seen one of the thick-billed finches picking at one end of a piece of cactus (which is in request among all the animals of the lower region), whilst a lizard was eating at the other; and afterwards the little bird with the utmost indifference hopped on the back of the reptile.

I opened the stomachs of several, and found them full of vegetable fibres, and leaves of different trees, especially of a species of acacia. In the upper region they live chiefly on the acid and astringent berries of the guayavita, under which trees I have seen these lizards and the huge tortoises feeding together. To obtain the acacia-leaves, they crawl up the low stunted trees; and it is not uncommon to see one or a pair quietly browsing, whilst seated on a branch several feet above the ground.

The meat of these animals when cooked is white, and by those whose stomachs rise above all prejudices, it is relished as very good food. Humboldt has remarked that in inter-tropical South America, all lizards which inhabit *dry* regions are esteemed delicacies for the table. The inhabitants say, that those inhabiting the damp region drink water, but that the others do not travel up for it from the sterile country like the tortoises. At the time of our visit, the females had within their bodies numerous large elongated eggs. These they lay in their burrows, and the inhabitants seek them for food.

These two species of Amblyrhyncus agree, as I have already stated, in general structure, and in many of their habits. Neither have that rapid movement, so characteristic of true Lacerta and Iguana. They are both herbivorous, although the kind of vegetation consumed in each case is so very different. Mr Bell has given the name to the genus from the shortness of the snout: indeed, the form of the mouth may almost be compared to that of the tortoise. One is tempted to suppose this is an adaptation to their herbivorous appetites. It is very interesting thus to find a well-characterized genus, having its aquatic and terrestrial species, belonging to so confined a portion of the world. The former species is by far the most remarkable, because it is the only existing Saurian, which can properly be said to be a maritime animal. I should perhaps have mentioned earlier, that in the whole archipelago, there is only one rill of fresh water that reaches the coast; yet these reptiles frequent the sea-beaches, and no other parts in all the islands. Moreover, there is no existing lizard, as far as I am aware, excepting this Amblyrhyncus, that feeds exclusively on aquatic productions. If, however, we refer to epochs long past, we shall find such habits common to several gigantic animals of the Saurian race.

To conclude with the order of reptiles. Of snakes there are several species, but all harmless. Of toads and frogs there are none. I was surprised at this, considering how well the temperate and damp woods in the elevated parts appeared adapted for their habits. It recalled to my mind the singular statement made by Bory St Vincent, namely, that none of this family are to be found on the volcanic islands in the great oceans. There certainly appears to be some foundation for this observation; which is the more remarkable, when compared with the case of lizards, which are generally among the earliest colonists of the smallest islet. It may be asked, whether this is not owing to the different facilities of transport through salt water, of the eggs of the latter protected by a calcareous coat, and of the slimy spawn of the former?

As I at first observed, these islands are not so remarkable for the number of species of reptiles, as for that of individuals; when we remember the well-beaten paths made by the many hundred great tortoises – the warrens of the terrestrial Amblyrhyncus – and the groups of the aquatic species basking on the coast-rocks – we must admit that there is no other quarter of the world, where this order replaces the herbivorous mammalia in so extraordinary a manner. It is worthy of observation by the geologist (who will probably refer back in his mind to the secondary periods, when the Saurians were developed with dimensions, which at the present day can be compared only to the cetaceous mammalia), that this archipelago, instead of possessing a humid climate and rank vegetation, cannot be considered otherwise than extremely arid, and for an equatorial region, remarkably temperate.

To finish with the zoology: I took great pains in collecting the insects, but I was surprised to find, even in the high and damp region, how exceedingly few they were in number. The forests of Tierra del Fuego are certainly much more barren; but with that exception I never collected in so poor a country. In the lower and sterile land I took seven species of Heteromera, and a few other insects; but in the fine thriving woods towards the centre of the islands, although I perseveringly swept under the bushes during all kinds of weather, I obtained only a few minute Diptera and Hymenoptera. Owing to this scarcity of insects, nearly all the birds live in the lower country; and the part which any one would have thought much the most favourable for them, is frequented only by a few of the small tyrant-flycatchers. I do not believe a single bird, excepting the water-rail, is confined to the damp region. Mr Waterhouse informs me that nearly all the insects belong to European forms, and that they do not by any means possess an equatorial character. I did not take a single one of large size, or of bright colours. This last observation applies equally to the birds and flowers. It is worthy of remark, that the only land-bird with bright colours, is that species of tyrant-flycatcher, which seems to be a wanderer from the continent. Of shells, there are a considerable number of land kinds, all of which, I believe are confined to this archipelago. Even of marine species, a large proportion were not known, before the collection made by Mr Cuming on these islands was brought to England.

I will not here attempt to come to any definite conclusions, as the species have not been accurately examined; but we may infer, that, with the exception of a few wanderers, the organic beings found on this archipelago are peculiar to it; and yet that their general form strongly partakes of an American character. It would be impossible for any one accustomed to the birds of Chile and La Plata to be placed on these islands, and not to feel convinced that he was, as far as the organic world was concerned, on American ground. This similarity in type, between distant islands and continents, while the species are distinct, has scarcely been sufficiently noticed. The circumstance would be explained, according to the views of some authors, by saying that the creative power had acted according to the same law over a wide area.

It has been mentioned, that the inhabitants can distinguish the tortoises, according to the islands whence they are brought. I was also informed that many of the islands possess trees and plants which do not occur on the others. For instance the berry-bearing tree, called Guayavita, which is common on James Island, certainly is not found on

Charles Island, though appearing equally well fitted for it. Unfortunately, I was not aware of these facts till my collection was nearly completed: it never occurred to me, that the productions of islands only a few miles apart, and placed under the same physical conditions, would be dissimilar. I therefore did not attempt to make a series of specimens from the separate islands. It is the fate of every voyager, when he has just discovered what object in any place is more particularly worthy of his attention, to be hurried from it. In the case of the mocking-bird, I ascertained (and have brought home the specimens) that one species (*Orpheus trifasciatus*, Gould) is exclusively found in Charles Island; a second (*O. parvulus*) on Albemarle Island; and a third (*O. melanotus*) common to James and Chatham Islands. The two last species are closely allied, but the first would be considered by every naturalist as quite distinct. I examined many specimens in the different islands, and in each the respective kind was *alone* present. These birds agree in general plumage, structure, and habits; so that the different species replace each other in the economy of the different islands. These species are not characterized by the markings on the plumage alone, but likewise by the size and form of the bill, and other differences. I have stated, that in the thirteen species of ground-finches, a nearly perfect gradation may be traced, from a beak extraordinarily thick, to one so fine, that it may be compared to that of a warbler. I very much suspect, that certain members of the series are confined to different islands; therefore, if the collection had been made on any *one* island, it would not have presented so perfect a gradation. It is clear, that if several islands have each their peculiar species of the same genera, when these are placed together, they will have a wide range of character. But there is not space in this work, to enter on this curious subject.

Before concluding my account of the zoology of these islands, I must describe more in detail the tameness of the birds. This disposition is common to all the terrestrial species; namely, to the mocking-birds, the finches, sylvicolæ, tyrant-flycatchers, doves, and hawks. There is not one which will not approach sufficiently near to be killed with a switch, and sometimes, as I have myself tried, with a cap or hat. A gun is here almost superfluous; for with the muzzle of one I pushed a hawk off the branch of a tree. One day a mocking-bird alighted on the edge of a pitcher (made of the shell of a tortoise), which I held in my hand whilst lying down. It began very quietly to sip the water, and allowed me to lift it with the vessel from the ground. I often tried, and very nearly succeeded, in catching these birds by their legs. Formerly the birds appear to have been even tamer than at present. Cowley (in the year 1684) says that the 'Turtle-doves were so tame that they would often alight upon our hats and arms, so as that we could take them alive: they not fearing man, until such time as some of our company did fire at them, whereby they were rendered more shy.' Dampier (in the same year) also says that a man in a morning's walk might kill six or seven dozen of these birds. At present, although certainly very tame, they do not alight on people's arms; nor do they suffer themselves to be killed in such numbers. It is surprising that the change has not been greater; for these islands during the last 150 years, have been frequently visited by bucaniers and whalers; and the sailors, wandering through the woods in search of tortoises, always take delight in knocking down the little birds.

These birds, although much persecuted, do not become wild in a short time: in Charles Island, which had then been colonized about six years, I saw a boy sitting by a well with a switch in his hand, with which he killed the doves and finches as they came to drink. He had already procured a little heap of them for his dinner; and he said he had constantly been in the habit of waiting there for the same purpose. We must conclude that the birds, not having as yet learnt that man is a more dangerous animal than the tortoise, or the Amblyrhyncus, disregard us, in the same manner as magpies in England do the cows and horses grazing in the fields.

The Falkland Islands offer a second instance of this disposition among its birds. The extraordinary tameness of the dark-coloured Furnarius has been remarked by Pernety, Lesson, and other voyagers. It is not, however, peculiar to that bird: the Caracara, snipe, upland and lowland goose, thrush, Emberiza, and even some true hawks, are all more or less tame. Both hawks and foxes are present; and as the birds are so tame, we may infer that the absence of all rapacious animals at the Galapagos, is not the cause of their tameness there. The geese at the Falklands, by the precaution they take in building on the islets, show that they are aware of their danger from the foxes; but they are not by this rendered wild towards man. This tameness of the birds, especially the waterfowl, is strongly contrasted with the habits of the same species in Tierra del Fuego, where for ages past they have been persecuted by the wild inhabitants. In the Falklands, the sportsman may sometimes kill more of the upland geese in one day, than he is able to carry home; whereas in Tierra del Fuego, it is nearly as difficult to kill one, as it is in England of the common wild species.

In the time of Pernety (1763), all the birds appear to have been much tamer than at present. Pernety states that the Furnarius would almost perch on his finger; and that with a wand he killed ten in half an hour. At that period, the birds must have been about as tame as they now are at the Galapagos. They appear to have learnt caution more quickly at the Falklands than at the latter place, and they have had proportionate means of experience; for besides frequent visits from vessels, the islands have been at intervals colonized during the whole period.

Even formerly, when all the birds were so tame, by Pernety's account it was impossible to kill the black-necked swan. It is rather an interesting fact, that this is a bird of passage, and therefore brings with it the wisdom learnt in foreign countries.

I have not met with any account of the *land* birds being so tame, in any other quarter of the world, as at the Galapagos and Falkland Islands. And it may be observed that of the few archipelagoes of any size, which when discovered were uninhabited by man, these two are among the most important. From the foregoing statements we may, I think, conclude; first, that the wildness of birds with regard to man, is a particular instinct directed against *him*, and not dependent on any general degree of caution arising from other sources of danger; secondly, that it is not acquired by them in a short time, even when much persecuted; but that in the course of successive generations it becomes hereditary. With domesticated animals we are accustomed to see instincts becoming hereditary; but with those in a state of nature, it is more rare to discover instances of such acquired knowledge. In regard to the wildness of birds towards men, there is no other way of accounting for it. Few young birds in England have been injured by man, yet all are afraid of him: many individuals, on the other hand, both at the Galapagos and at the Falklands, have been injured, but yet have not learned that salutary dread. We may infer from these facts, what havoc the introduction of any new beast of prey must cause in a country, before the instincts of the aborigines become adapted to the stranger's craft or power.

Tahiti

Tahiti – Aspect – Vegetation on the slope of the
mountains – View of Eimeo – Excursion in the interior – Profound
ravines – Succession of waterfalls – Number of wild useful
plants – Temperance of inhabitants – Their moral state –
Parliament convened

OCTOBER 20TH – The survey of the Galapagos Archipelago being concluded, a course was steered towards Tahiti; and we commenced our long passage of 3,200 miles. In the course of a few days we sailed out of the gloomy and clouded region, which extends during the winter far from the coast of South America. We then enjoyed bright and clear weather, while running pleasantly along at the rate of 150 or 160 miles a day before a steady trade wind. The temperature in this more central part of the Pacific, is higher than near the American shore. The thermometer in the poop cabin, both by night and day, ranged between 80° and 83°, which to my feelings was quite delightful; but with one degree higher, the effect became oppressive. We passed through the Dangerous or Low Archipelago, and saw several of those most curious rings of land, just rising above the edge of the water, which have been called Lagoon Islands. A long and brilliantly white beach is capped by a margin of green vegetation;

and this strip appears on both hands rapidly to narrow away in the distance, and then sinks beneath the horizon. From the mast-head a wide expanse of smooth water can be seen within the annular margin of land. These low islands bear no proportion to the vast ocean out of which they abruptly rise; and it seems wonderful, that such weak intruders are not overwhelmed, by the all-powerful and never-tiring waves of that great sea, miscalled the Pacific.

NOVEMBER 15TH – At daylight, Tahiti, an island which must for ever remain as classical to the voyager in the South Sea, was in view. At this distance the appearance was not very inviting. The luxuriant vegetation of the lower parts was not discernible, and as the clouds rolled past, the wildest and most precipitous peaks showed themselves towards the centre of the island. As soon as we came to an anchor in Matavai Bay, we were surrounded by canoes. This was our Sunday, but the Monday of Tahiti: if the case had been reversed, we should not have received a single visit; for the injunction not to launch a canoe on the sabbath is rigidly obeyed. After dinner we landed to enjoy all the delights of the first impressions produced by a new country, and that country the charming Tahiti. A crowd of men, women, and children, was collected on the memorable Point Venus, ready to receive us with laughing, merry faces. They marshalled us towards the house of Mr Wilson, the missionary of the district, who met us on the road, and gave us a very friendly reception. After sitting a short time in his house, we separated to walk about, but returned there in the evening.

The land capable of cultivation is scarcely in any part more than a fringe of low alluvial soil, accumulated round the base of the mountains, and protected from the waves of the sea by a coral reef, which encircles at a distance the entire line of coast. The reef is broken in several parts so that ships can pass through, and the lake of smooth water within thus affords a safe harbour, as well as a channel for the native canoes. The low land which comes down to the beach of coral sand, is covered by the most beautiful productions of the inter-tropical regions. In the midst of bananas, orange, cocoa-nut, and breadfruit trees, spots are cleared where yams, sweet potatoes, sugar-cane, and pine-apples, are cultivated. Even the brushwood is a fruit-tree, namely, the guava, which from its abundance is as noxious as a weed. In Brazil I have often admired the contrast of varied beauty in the banana, palm, and orange-tree: here we have in addition the breadfruit, conspicuous from its large, glossy, and deeply digitated leaf. It is admirable to behold groves of a tree, sending forth its branches with the force of an English oak, loaded with large and most nutritious fruit. However little on most occasions utility explains the delight received from any fine prospect, in this case it cannot fail to enter as an element in the feeling. The little winding paths, cool from the surrounding shade, led to the scattered houses; and the owners of these every where gave us a cheerful and most hospitable reception.

I was pleased with nothing so much as with the inhabitants. There is a mildness in the expression of their countenances, which at once banishes the idea of a savage; and an intelligence, which shows they are advancing in civilization. Their dress is as yet incongruous; no settled costume having taken the place of the ancient one. But even in its present state, it is far from being so ridiculous as it has been described by travellers of a few years' standing. Those who can afford it wear a white shirt, and sometimes a jacket, with a wrapper of coloured cotton round their middles; thus making a short petticoat, like the chilipa of the Gauchos. This dress appears so general with the chiefs, that it will probably become the settled fashion. No one, even to the queen, wears shoes or stockings; and only the chiefs have a straw hat on their heads. The common people, when working, keep the upper part of their bodies uncovered; and it is then that the Tahitians are seen to advantage. They are very tall, broad-shouldered, athletic and with well-proportioned limbs. It has been somewhere remarked, that it requires little habit to make a darker tint of the skin more pleasing and natural, even to the eye of an European, than his own colour. To see a white man bathing by the side of a Tahitian, was like comparing a plant bleached by the gardener's art, with one growing in the open fields. Most of the men are tattooed; and the ornaments follow the curvature of the body so gracefully, that they have a very pleasing and elegant effect. One common figure, varying only in its detail, branches somewhat like a tuft of palm-leaves from the line of the back-bone, and curls round each side. The simile may be a fanciful one, but I thought the body of a man thus ornamented, was like the trunk of a noble tree embraced by a delicate creeper.

Many of the older people had their feet covered with small figures, placed in order so as to resemble a sock. This fashion, however, is partly gone by, and has been succeeded by others. Here, although each man must for ever abide by the whim which reigned in his early days, yet fashion is far from immutable. An old man has thus his age for ever stamped on his body, and he cannot assume the airs of a young dandy. The women are also tattooed in the same manner as the men, and very commonly on their fingers. An unbecoming fashion in one respect is now almost universal: it is that of cutting the hair, or rather shaving it, from the upper part of the head, in a circular form, so as to leave only an outer ring of hair. The missionaries have tried to persuade the people to change this habit: but it is the fashion, and that is sufficient answer at Tahiti as well as at Paris. I was much disappointed in the personal appearance of the women; they are far inferior in every respect to the men. The custom of wearing a flower in the back of the head, or through a small hole in each ear, is pretty; the flower is generally either white or scarlet, and like the Camelia Japonica. They wear also a sort of crown of woven cocoa-nut leaves, as a shade to their eyes. The women appear to be in greater want of some becoming costume, even than the men.

Nearly all understand a little English; that is, they know the names of common things, and by the aid of this, together with signs, a lame sort of conversation could be carried on. In returning in the evening to the boat, we stopped to witness a very pretty scene; numbers of children were playing on the beach, and had lighted bonfires, which illuminated the placid sea and surrounding trees. Others, in circles, were singing Tahitian verses. We seated ourselves on the sand, and joined their party. The songs were impromptu, and I believe related to our arrival: one little girl sang a line, which the rest took up in parts, forming a very pretty chorus. The whole scene made us unequivocally aware that we were seated on the shores of an island in the South Sea.

NOVEMBER 18TH – In the morning I came on shore early, bringing with me some provisions in a bag, and two blankets for myself and servant. These were lashed to each end of a pole, and thus carried by my Tahitian companions: from custom these men are able to walk for a whole day, with as much as 50 pounds at each end. I told my guides to provide themselves with food and clothing: but for the latter, they said their skins were sufficient, and for the former, that there was plenty of food in the mountains. The line of march was the valley of Tia-auru, in which the river flows that enters the sea by Point Venus. This is one of the principal streams in the island, and its source lies at the base of the loftiest pinnacles, which attain the elevation of about 7,000 feet. The whole island may be considered as one group of mountains, so that the only way to penetrate the interior is to follow up the valleys. Our road, at first, lay through the wood which bordered each side of the river; and the glimpses of the lofty central peaks, seen as through an avenue, with here and there a waving cocoa-nut tree on one side, were extremely picturesque. The valley soon began to narrow, and the sides to grow lofty and more precipitous. After having walked between three and four hours, we found the width of the ravine scarcely exceeded that of the bed of the stream. On each hand the walls were nearly vertical; yet from the soft nature of the volcanic strata, trees and a rank vegetation sprung from every projecting ledge. These precipices must have been some 1,000 feet high: and the whole formed a mountain gorge, far more magnificent than any thing which I had ever before beheld. Until the mid-day sun stood vertically over the ravine, the air had felt cool and damp, but now it became very sultry. Shaded by a ledge of rock, beneath a façade of columnar lava, we ate our dinner. My guides had already procured a dish of small fish and fresh-water prawns. They carried with them a small net stretched on a hoop; and where the water was deep and in eddies, they dived, and like otters, by their eyesight followed the fish into holes and corners, and thus secured them.

The Tahitians have the dexterity of amphibious animals in the water. An anecdote mentioned by Ellis shows how much they feel at home in that element. When a horse was landing for Pomarre in 1817, the slings broke, and it fell into the water: immediately the natives jumped overboard, and by their cries and vain efforts at assistance, almost drowned the animal. As soon, however, as it reached the shore, the whole population took to flight, and tried to hide themselves from the man-carrying-pig, as they christened the horse.

A little higher up, the river divided itself into three little streams. The two northern ones were impracticable, owing to a succession of waterfalls, which descended from the jagged summit of the highest mountain; the other to all appearance was equally inaccessible, but we managed to ascend it by a most extraordinary road. The sides of the valley were here nearly precipitous; but, as frequently happens with stratified rocks, small ledges projected, which were thickly covered by wild bananas, liliaceous plants, and other luxuriant productions of the tropics. The Tahitians, by climbing amongst these ledges, searching for fruit, had discovered a track by which the whole precipice could be scaled. The first ascent from the valley was very dangerous: for it was necessary to pass the face of a naked rock, by the aid of ropes, which we brought with us. How any person discovered that this formidable spot was the only point where the side of the mountain was practicable, I cannot imagine. We then cautiously walked along one of the ledges, till we came to the stream already alluded to. This ledge formed a flat spot, above which a beautiful cascade, of some 100 feet, poured down its waters, and beneath it another high one emptied itself into the main stream. From this cool and shady recess, we made a circuit to avoid the overhanging cascade. As before, we followed little projecting ledges, the apparent danger being partly hidden by the thickness of the vegetation. In passing from one of the ledges to another, there was a vertical wall of rock. One of the Tahitians, a fine active man, placed the trunk of a tree against this, climbed up it, and then by the aid of crevices reached the summit. He fixed the ropes to a projecting point, and lowered them for us, then hauled up a dog which accompanied us, and lastly our luggage. Beneath the ledge on which the dead tree was placed the precipice must have been 500 or 600 feet deep; and if the abyss had not been partly concealed by the overhanging ferns and lilies, my head would have turned giddy, and nothing should have induced me to have attempted it. We continued to ascend sometimes along ledges, and sometimes along knife-edged ridges, having on each hand profound ravines. In the Cordillera, I have seen mountains on a far grander scale, but for abruptness, no part of them at all comparable to this. In the evening we reached a flat little spot on the banks of the same stream, which I have mentioned as descending by a chain of waterfalls. Here we bivouacked for the night. On each side of the ravine there were great beds of the Feyé, or mountain-banana, covered with ripe fruit. Many of these plants were from 20 to 25 feet high, and from 3 to 4 in circumference. By the aid of strips of bark for twine, the stems of bamboos for rafters, and the large leaf of the banana for a thatch, the Tahitians in a few minutes built an excellent house; and with the withered leaves made a soft bed.

They then proceeded to make a fire, and cook our evening meal. A light was procured by rubbing a blunt-pointed stick in a groove made in another (as if with the intention of deepening it), until by friction the dust became ignited. A peculiarly white and very light wood (the *Hibiscus tiliaceus*) is alone used for this purpose: it is the same which serves for poles to carry any burden, and for the floating outrigger to steady the canoe. The fire was produced in a few seconds: but, to a person who does not understand the art, it requires the greatest exertion; as I found, before at last, to my great pride, I succeeded in igniting the dust. The Gaucho in the Pampas uses a different method: taking an elastic stick about 18 inches long, he presses one end on his breast, and the other (which is pointed) in a hole in a piece of wood, and then rapidly turns the curved part, like a carpenter's centre-bit. The Tahitians having made a small fire of sticks, placed a score of stones, of about the size of cricket-balls, on the burning wood. In about ten minutes' time the sticks were consumed and the stones hot. They had previously folded up in small parcels of leaves, pieces of beef, fish, ripe and unripe bananas, and the tops of the wild arum. These green parcels were laid in a layer between two layers of the hot stones, and the whole then covered up with earth, so that no smoke or steam could escape. In about a quarter of an hour, the whole was most deliciously cooked. The choice green parcels were now laid on a cloth of banana-leaves, and with a cocoa-nut shell we drank the cool water of the running stream and thus we enjoyed our rustic meal.

I could not look on the surrounding plants without admiration. On every side were forests of banana; the fruit of which, though serving for food in various ways, lay in heaps decaying on the ground. In front of us there was an extensive brake of wild sugar-cane; and the stream was shaded by the dark green knotted stem of the ava – so famous in former days for its powerful intoxicating effects. I chewed a piece, and found that it had an acrid and unpleasant taste, which would have induced any one at once to have pronounced it poisonous. Thanks be to the missionaries, this plant now thrives only in these deep ravines, innocuous to every one. Close by I saw the wild arum, the roots of which, when well baked, are good to eat, and the young leaves better than spinach. There was the wild yam, and a liliaceous plant called Ti, which grows in abundance, and has a soft brown root, in shape and size like a huge log of wood. This served us for dessert, for it is as sweet as treacle, and with a pleasant taste. There were, moreover, several other wild fruits, and useful vegetables. The little stream, besides its cool water, produced eels and cray-fish. I did indeed admire this scene, when I compared it with an uncultivated one in the temperate zones. I felt the force of the observation, that man, at least savage man, with his reasoning powers only partly developed, is the child of the tropics.

As the evening drew to a close, I strolled beneath the gloomy shade of the bananas up the course of the stream. My walk was soon brought to a close, by coming to a waterfall between 200 and 300 feet high; and again above this there was another. I mention all these waterfalls in this one brook, to give a general idea of the inclination of the land. In the little recess where the water fell, it did not appear that a breath of wind had ever entered. The leaves of the banana, damp with spray, possessed an unbroken edge, instead of being split, as generally is the case, into a thousand shreds. From our position, almost suspended on the mountain-side, there were glimpses into the depths of the neighbouring valleys; and the lofty points of the central mountains, towering up within 60° of the zenith, hid half the evening sky. Thus seated, it was a sublime spectacle to watch the shades of night gradually obscuring the last and highest pinnacles.

Before we laid ourselves down to sleep, the elder Tahitian fell on his knees, and with closed eyes repeated a long prayer in his native tongue. He prayed as a Christian should do, with fitting reverence, and without the fear of ridicule or any ostentation of piety. At our meals neither of the men would taste food, without saying beforehand a short grace. Those travellers, who think that a Tahitian prays only when the eyes of the missionary are fixed on him, should have slept with us that night on the mountain-side. Before morning it rained very heavily; but the good thatch of banana-leaves kept us dry.

NOVEMBER 19TH — At daylight my friends, after their morning prayer, prepared an excellent breakfast in the same manner as in the evening. They themselves certainly partook of it largely; indeed I never saw any men eat nearly so much. I should suppose such capacious stomachs must be the result of a large part of their diet consisting of fruit and vegetables, which contain, in a given bulk, a comparatively small portion of nutriment. Unwittingly, I was the means of my companions breaking (as I afterwards learned) one of their own laws and resolutions. I took with me a flask of spirits, which they could not resolve to refuse; but as often as they drank a little, they put their fingers before their mouths, and uttered the word 'Missionary'. About two years ago, although the use of the ava was prevented, drunkenness from the introduction of spirits became very prevalent. The missionaries prevailed on a few good men, who saw their country rapidly going to ruin, to join with them in a Temperance Society. From good sense or shame all the chiefs and the queen were at last persuaded to join it. Immediately a law was passed that no spirits should be allowed to be introduced into the island, and that he who sold and he who bought the forbidden article, should be punished by a fine. With remarkable justice, a certain period was allowed for stock in hand to be sold, before the law came into effect. But when it did, a general search was made in which even the houses of the missionaries were not exempted, and all the ava (as the natives call all ardent spirits) was poured on the ground. When one reflects on the effect of intemperance on the aborigines of the two Americas, I think it will be acknowledged, that every well-wisher of Tahiti owes no common debt of gratitude to the missionaries. As long as the little island of St Helena remained under the government of the East India Company, spirits, owing to the great injury they had produced, were not allowed to be imported; but wine was supplied from the Cape of Good Hope. It is rather a striking, and not very gratifying fact, that in the same year that spirits were allowed to be sold on that island, their use was banished from Tahiti by the free will of the people.

After breakfast we proceeded on our journey. As my object was merely to see a little of the interior scenery, we returned by another track, which descended into the main valley lower down. For some distance we wound, by a most intricate path, along the side of the mountain which formed the valley. In the less precipitous parts we passed through extensive groves of the wild banana. The Tahitians, with their naked, tattooed bodies, their heads ornamented with flowers, and seen in the dark shade of the woods, would have formed a fine picture of man, inhabiting some primeval forest. In our descent we followed the line of ridges; these were exceedingly narrow, and for considerable lengths steep as a ladder; but all clothed with vegetation. The extreme care necessary in poising

47

each step rendered the walk fatiguing. I am never weary of expressing my astonishment at these ravines and precipices: the mountains may almost be described, as rent by so many crevices. When viewing the surrounding country from the knife-edged ridges, the point of support was so small, that the effect was nearly the same, I should think, as from a balloon. In this descent we had occasion to use the ropes only once, at the point where we entered the main valley. We slept under the same ledge of rock, where, the day before, we had dined: the night was fine, but from the depth and narrowness of the gorge, profoundly dark.

Before actually seeing this country, I had difficulty in understanding two facts mentioned by Ellis; namely, that after the murderous battles of former times, the survivors on the conquered side retired into the mountains, where a handful of men could resist a multitude. Certainly half a dozen men, at the spot where the Tahitian reared the old tree, could easily have repulsed thousands. Secondly, that after the introduction of Christianity, there were wild men who lived in the mountains, and whose retreats were unknown to the more civilized inhabitants.

NOVEMBER 20TH — In the morning we started early, and reached Matavai at noon. On the road we met a large party of noble athletic men, going for wild bananas. I found that the ship, on account of the difficulty in watering, had moved to the harbour of Papawa, to which place I immediately walked. This is a very pretty spot. The cove is

48

surrounded by reefs, and the water as smooth as that in a lake. The cultivated ground, with all its beautiful productions, and the cottages, comes close down to the water's edge.

From the varying accounts which I had read before reaching these islands, I was very anxious to form, from my own observation, a judgment of their moral state – although such judgment would necessarily be very imperfect. A first impression at all times very much depends on one's previously acquired ideas. My notions were drawn from Ellis's *Polynesian Researches* – an admirable and most interesting work, but naturally looking at every thing under a favourable point of view; from Beechey's *Voyage* and from that of Kotzebue, which is strongly adverse to the whole missionary system. He who compares these three accounts, will, I think, form a tolerably accurate conception of the present state of Tahiti. One of my impressions, which I took from the two last authorities, was decidedly incorrect; viz., that the Tahitians had become a gloomy race, and lived in fear of the missionaries. Of the latter feeling I saw no trace, unless, indeed, fear and respect be confounded under one name. Instead of discontent being a common feeling, it would be difficult in Europe to pick out of a crowd half so many merry and happy faces. The prohibition of the flute and dancing is inveighed against as wrong and foolish; the more than Presbyterian manner of keeping the sabbath, is looked at in a similar light. On these points I will not pretend to offer any opinion in opposition to men who have resided as many years as I was days on the island.

On the whole it appears to me, that the morality and religion of the inhabitants is highly creditable. There are many who attack, even more acrimoniously than Kotzebue, both the missionaries, their system, and the effects produced by it. Such reasoners never compare the present state with that of the island only twenty years ago; nor even with that of Europe at this day; but they compare it with the high standard of Gospel perfection. They expect the missionaries to effect that, which the Apostles themselves failed to do. In as much as the condition of the people falls short of this high order, blame is attached to the missionary, instead of credit for that which he has effected. They forget, or will not remember, that human sacrifices, and the power of an idolatrous priesthood – a system of profligacy unparalleled in the world, and infanticide a consequence on that system – bloody wars, where the conquerors spared neither women nor children – that all these have been abolished; and that dishonesty, intemperance, and licentiousness have been greatly reduced by the introduction of Christianity. In a voyager to forget these things is base ingratitude; for should he chance to be at the point of shipwreck on some unknown coast, he will most devoutly pray that the lesson of the missionary may be found to have extended thus far.

In point of morality the virtue of the women, it has been often said, is most open to exception. But before they are blamed too severely, it will be well distinctly to call to mind the scenes described by Captain Cook and Mr Banks, in which the grandmothers and mothers of the present race played a part. Those who are most severe, should consider how much of the morality of the women in Europe is owing to the system early impressed by mothers on their daughters, and how much in each individual case to the precepts of religion. But it is useless to argue against such reasoners: I believe that disappointed in not finding the field of licentiousness quite so open as formerly, they will not give credit to a morality which they do not wish to practise, or to a religion which they undervalue, if not despise.

SUNDAY 22ND – The harbour of Papiete, which may be considered as the capital of the island, is about 7 miles distant from Matavai, to which point the *Beagle* had returned. The queen resides there, and it is the seat of government, and the chief resort of shipping. Captain FitzRoy took a party there to hear divine service, first in the Tahitian language, and afterwards in our own. Mr Pritchard, the leading missionary in the island, performed the service, which was a most interesting spectacle. The chapel consisted of a large airy framework of wood; and it was filled to excess by tidy, clean people, of all ages and both sexes. I was rather disappointed in the apparent degree of attention; but I believe my expectations were raised too high. At all events the appearance was quite equal to that in a country church in England. The singing of the hymns was decidedly very pleasing; but the language from the pulpit, although fluently delivered, did not sound well. A constant repetition of words, like '*tata ta, mata mai*', rendered it monotonous. After English service, a party returned on foot to Matavai. It was a pleasant walk, sometimes along the sea-beach and sometimes under the shade of the many beautiful trees.

About two years ago, a small vessel under English colours was plundered by the inhabitants of the Low Islands, which were then under the dominion of the Queen of Tahiti. It was believed that the perpetrators were instigated to this act by some indiscreet laws issued by her majesty. The British government demanded compensation; which was acceded to, and a sum of nearly $3,000 was agreed to be paid on the first of last September. The commodore at Lima ordered Captain FitzRoy, to inquire concerning this debt, and to demand satisfaction if it were not paid. Captain FitzRoy accordingly requested an interview with the queen: and a parliament was held to consider the question; at which all the principal chiefs of the island and the queen were assembled. I will not attempt to describe what took place, after the interesting account given by Captain FitzRoy. The money it appeared had not been paid. Perhaps the alleged reasons for the failure were rather equivocating: but otherwise I cannot sufficiently express our general surprise, at the extreme good sense, the reasoning powers, moderation, candour, and prompt resolution, which were displayed on all sides. I believe every one of us left the meeting with a very different opinion of the Tahitians, from that which we entertained when entering. The chiefs and people resolved to subscribe and complete the sum which was wanting: Captain FitzRoy urged that it was hard that their private property should be sacrificed for the crimes of distant islanders. They replied, that they were grateful for his consideration, but that Pomarre was their queen, and they were determined to help her in this her difficulty. This resolution and its prompt execution (for a book was opened early the next morning), made a perfect conclusion to this very remarkable scene of loyalty and good feeling.

After the main discussion was ended, several of the chiefs took the opportunity of asking Captain FitzRoy many intelligent questions, concerning international customs and laws. These related to the treatment of ships and foreigners. On some points, as soon as the decision was made, the law was issued verbally on the spot. This Tahitian parliament lasted for several hours; and when it was over Captain FitzRoy invited the queen to pay the *Beagle* a visit.

NOVEMBER 26TH — In the evening, with a gentle land-breeze, a course was steered for New Zealand, and as the sun set we took a farewell look at the mountains of Tahiti — the island to which every voyager has offered up his tribute of admiration.

PENGUIN 60s CLASSICS

PENGUIN 60S CLASSICS

HENRY JAMES · *The Lesson of the Master*
FRANZ KAFKA · *The Judgement* and *In the Penal Colony*
THOMAS À KEMPIS · *Counsels on the Spiritual Life*
HEINRICH VON KLEIST · *The Marquise of O—*
LIVY · *Hannibal's Crossing of the Alps*
NICCOLÒ MACHIAVELLI · *The Art of War*
SIR THOMAS MALORY · *The Death of King Arthur*
GUY DE MAUPASSANT · *Boule de Suif*
FRIEDRICH NIETZSCHE · *Zarathustra's Discourses*
OVID · *Orpheus in the Underworld*
PLATO · *Phaedrus*
EDGAR ALLAN POE · *The Murders in the Rue Morgue*
ARTHUR RIMBAUD · *A Season in Hell*
JEAN-JACQUES ROUSSEAU · *Meditations of a Solitary Walker*
ROBERT LOUIS STEVENSON · *Dr Jekyll and Mr Hyde*
TACITUS · *Nero and the Burning of Rome*
HENRY DAVID THOREAU · *Civil Disobedience* and *Reading*
LEO TOLSTOY · *The Death of Ivan Ilyich*
IVAN TURGENEV · *Three Sketches from a Hunter's Album*
MARK TWAIN · *The Man That Corrupted Hadleyburg*
GIORGIO VASARI · *Lives of Three Renaissance Artists*
EDITH WHARTON · *Souls Belated*
WALT WHITMAN · *Song of Myself*
OSCAR WILDE · *The Portrait of Mr W. H.*

ANONYMOUS WORKS

Beowulf and Grendel
Buddha's Teachings
Gilgamesh and Enkidu

Krishna's Dialogue on the Soul
Tales of Cú Chulaind
Two Viking Romances

READ MORE IN PENGUIN

For complete information about books available from Penguin and how to order them, please write to us at the appropriate address below. Please note that for copyright reasons the selection of books varies from country to country.

IN THE UNITED KINGDOM: Please write to *Dept. EP, Penguin Books Ltd, Bath Road, Harmondsworth, Middlesex UB7 0DA.*

IN THE UNITED STATES: Please write to *Consumer Sales, Penguin USA, P.O. Box 999, Dept. 17109, Bergenfield, New Jersey 07621-0120.* VISA and MasterCard holders call 1-800-253-6476 to order Penguin titles.

IN CANADA: Please write to *Penguin Books Canada Ltd, 10 Alcorn Avenue, Suite 300, Toronto, Ontario M4V 3B2.*

IN AUSTRALIA: Please write to *Penguin Books Australia Ltd, P.O. Box 257, Ringwood, Victoria 3134.*

IN NEW ZEALAND: Please write to *Penguin Books (NZ) Ltd, Private Bag 102902, North Shore Mail Centre, Auckland 10.*

IN INDIA: Please write to *Penguin Books India Pvt Ltd, 706 Eros Apartments, 56 Nehru Place, New Delhi 110 019.*

IN THE NETHERLANDS: Please write to *Penguin Books Netherlands bv, Postbus 3507, NL-1001 AH Amsterdam.*

IN GERMANY: Please write to *Penguin Books Deutschland GmbH, Metzlerstrasse 26, 60594 Frankfurt am Main.*

IN SPAIN: Please write to *Penguin Books S. A., Bravo Murillo 19, 1° B, 28015 Madrid.*

IN ITALY: Please write to *Penguin Italia s.r.l., Via Felice Casati 20, I-20124 Milano.*

IN FRANCE: Please write to *Penguin France S. A., 17 rue Lejeune, F-31000 Toulouse.*

IN JAPAN: Please write to *Penguin Books Japan, Ishikiribashi Building, 2-5-4, Suido, Bunkyo-ku, Tokyo 112.*

IN GREECE: Please write to *Penguin Hellas Ltd, Dimocritou 3, GR-106 71 Athens.*

IN SOUTH AFRICA: Please write to *Longman Penguin Southern Africa (Pty) Ltd, Private Bag X08, Bertsham 2013.*